What you need to know to invest with confidence

"I did it starting as a poor African immigrant, and so can you"

© 2009 by Mati Ntongondu

TABLE OF CONTENTS

FOREWORD

Having worked in almost all real estate related fields, I know that many people in these professions work very hard and I do not want to appear to be stepping on anybody's toes.

My intention is to teach you the correct principles so you can protect yourself out there and avoid getting ripped off. This information will also enable you to be informed so you can have more meaningful conversations with your lender, realtor, property manager and other professionals you will be dealing with. This is a starting point, and does not in any way replace your trusted advisors.

I am not an Accountant or Attorney. I highly advise that you consult these professionals on the implication of any investments you intend to pursue.

The information in this book will equip you with the knowledge of how to utilize your team members or advisors for maximum benefit. I have found that, when you are knowledgeable, your advisors give you better information because they just can't fool you. When you have no clue, they can only give you the basics because they figure you don't have the capacity to assimilate the real thing.

This book will give you real world information you need to invest with confidence. It is written not from the theory or academic point of view, but from the practical standpoint on how to invest in a smart way from someone who has invested and is still investing in real estate.

Education makes you powerful. It is one of the only things that nobody can take away from you. I encourage you to read other real estate books, associate with other investors, attend training, and do all you can to build on your knowledge so you can become an even better investor.

Even more important, though, is taking action. Great ideas will remain just that unless acted upon. You must make it a habit to put to practical use what you learn or it will be of no benefit to you. All the courses in the world will never yield a penny until you take action to apply the knowledge you've gained.

INTRODUCTION

I am an absolute believer in the declaration KNOWLEDGE IS POWER. When you know what you are doing, people don't mess with you. You also get better advice from professionals

because they know they can't just give you bogus information because you are sharp.

Here is where I am coming from. In 1999 my wife and I got taken advantage of in the worst way because I did not know what I was doing. We were living with in-laws, having just moved back to Utah from California. We had overstayed our welcome and were desperate to get into a home of our own.

We were introduced to George, a loan officer from hell, who started seeing dollar signs the first time he talked to us. We made it very clear that that we had to get a home of our own and we had no clue what we were doing because we had never bought a house before. He promptly instructed us to find a house and he would take care of all the details. We found a great home in Riverton, negotiated a great deal, and George helped us write up the offer.

We told him that the most we could afford was a maximum of $1,000 a month; he said that was not a problem. I called him a couple of times to check how everything was going, and he assured me that we would get the house. George would call and coach me on what to say minutes before I got calls from lenders. I just thought this was standard procedure in getting a loan. In hindsight, I was really participating in fraud without knowing it.

The last time we heard from George, he gave us the great news that the loan would close the following day. We went to the title company and there was no George. I was very nervous because I had never been to a title company before, and the only person who was supposed to be looking out for us was a no show. When the escrow officer brought out the paperwork and started to go over the HUD 1 Statement, we knew we were in trouble. The principal and interest payment was $1,385. We weren't happy that the payment was $385 more than we could afford every month. Nobody bothered to explain that we would also be responsible for paying taxes and insurance. The escrow officer just shoved the papers in front of us and told us to sign. We signed the papers because refusing to sign meant going back to live with the in-laws. I had put my pride on the line a little bit, because I had told a few people that we were moving up in the world and getting a place of our own.

Anyway, this was in September, and in a few months, we found that the mortgage company got forced insurance (home owners insurance) on our behalf which was about twice what it was supposed to cost. We had to pay the entire annual premium right away, and that was painful. Then, in November, we got the shock of our lives, when we got the tax bill which had to be paid before the end of that month, or the state would file a tax lien on our home. This was the beginning of our financial troubles that resulted in a Chapter 7 Bankruptcy.

We got in trouble because the mortgage payment was too high and, in order to make things work, we had to stop paying other bills. My beloved Subaru Legacy was repossessed and our credit went to pot. At last we just had no choice but to go bankrupt. This did a number on my self-esteem and it was very tough on us. We tried to hide this from our family and friends for a very long time.

After this happened to us, I swore I would study and understand the mortgage process so nobody would ever take advantage of me again. I also wanted to help as many people as I could not to go through what I had gone through. I got a job as a mortgage loan officer and eventually started my own mortgage company. I worked very hard to help many people in getting both purchase or refinance loans. I eventually closed Personal Advantage Mortgage after I got more involved in investing.

I am telling you all this to emphasize the need for knowing what you are doing. Had we known the right questions to ask, we would not have been burned. This was a very expensive lesson to learn, and it took me many years to straighten out my credit profile.

Chapter1: DEVELOPING A WINNER MINDSET

Reading real estate/self improvement books

When I graduated from engineering school, my brain was so burned out that I swore I would never read a book again in my entire life. I was true to my commitment for a couple of years until I became friends with a good neighbor in Walnut Creek California, who talked me into going through a real estate home study course he had bought. It was the Carleton Sheet's 'No Money Down' course, and I was intrigued by the concepts he was sharing. My friend and I would take turns going to each other's apartments to listen to the CDs and read the manual together. It took us about 3 weeks to get through the course, and we were so excited to finish it so we could get started.

One of the first action items after you completed the course was to introduce yourself to title/ escrow companies. I had never in my entire life heard the word 'escrow' before and, although my friend was a little smarter than myself, we did not know where to begin. We looked at each other, and said, "Forget it; this is way over our heads." Just like that, we gave up, but a seed had been planted in my mind of the great possibilities in real estate investing.

One of the major underlying issues for me is that I suffered from an inferiority complex. I had always considered myself a small village boy from Kenya and American real estate was just too much for my little brain to comprehend.

About the same time, I was introduced by a friend to AMWAY and, although I never built an organization, I was introduced to some great books. I stuck around for a while because of the self-improvement I was experiencing through books and tapes. For me, it was just what the doctor ordered. This was the beginning of my love of self-improvement. Here are some of the best books I have read on self-improvement, and I would recommend you looking into them. These books have literally changed my life.

1. *How to Win Friends and Influence People*, by Dale Carnegie

2. *The Richest Man in Babylon*, by George S. Clason

3. *How I Raised Myself From Failure to Success Through Selling*, by Frank Betger

4. *As a Man Thinketh*, by James Allen

5. *Being Happy*, by Andrew Matthews

6. *Think and Grow Rich*, by Napoleon Hill

7. *The Power of Positive Thinking*, by Norman Vincent Peale

8. *How to Have Confidence and Power in Dealing with People*, by Les Giblin

9. Books by Tony Robins

10. Books by Robert T. Kiyosaki

Here are also some of the best books I have read on real estate investing:

1. *No Money Down,* by Robert Allen

2. *The Art of The Deal*, by Donald Trump

3. *Real Estate Riches*, by Dolf De Roos

4. *Making Money in Real Estate*, by Dolf De Roos

5. *Real Estate Investing Loopholes*, Dolf De Roos

6. *The ABC's of Real Estate Investing*, Ken McElrol

7. *The ABC's of Real Estate Management*, Ken McElroy

8. *The Advanced Guide to Real Estate Investing*, by Ken McElroy

9. Books by Wright Thurston

10. *Lease Options & Subject To*, by Wendy Patton

Listen to tapes/CDs

For the past 14 years, I have always listened to tapes or CDs whenever I drive anywhere for more than 15 minutes, except during the holidays because I love listening to Christmas music on the radio. I don't sweat bad traffic because it means more learning time for me. I also allow myself one news update a day just to know what is going on. As you know, after you listen to half hour of radio, it is pretty much the same stories repeated all day. Also, next time you listen to the radio, pay attention to the content. It seems to me as though more than 90% of news is about murders and crimes. In my humble opinion, news is so negative that it is not worth my time.

Turn your car into a 'University on Wheels' by sticking in a tape cassette or CD when you commute. You will be surprised how much good material you can cover in a week just commuting between home and work. Most of the books I read I also have on CD. My favorite section at the bookstore is the audio book section.

Try an experiment; listen to self-improvement real estate tapes of CDs during your commute for one full week. After that, listen to the radio, and you will be surprised at how negative news really is. You can get a lot of good material from your local library for free.

Join a local investment club or Apartment Association & network

If I asked any parent if they think whoever their kids hang out with influence them – either for the better or worse – I know the answer would be a definite yes. The power of association is as important to adults as it is to our kids.

Joining and participating in your local investors club or Apartment Association is a great way to associate with people who have the same interests. People who attend these clubs and associations are fellow landlords, property managers, investors, hard and private money lenders, mortgage brokers, real estate agents, escrow officers, appraisers, real estate attorneys, plumbers, handymen, bookkeepers, accountants, etc. These are the types of people you need to know if you are going to do anything in real estate.

Apartment Associations are a wealth of information on legal issues related to land lording including tenant and property owner rights. This is of utmost importance if you are going to be involved with rentals. If you want to stay informed on what is going on in your market, your area Apartment Association is a great place to be. These clubs and associations bring in speakers who teach on various topics of interest to real estate field. If you attend regularly, you will get educated by professionals with real world experience, as opposed to reading the information from a book. Some of the speakers are there to promote their businesses and would take time to meet with you at their office for free, just for the asking. Remember, they want you as their client, but don't think they will spend days teaching you. If you have done your homework and read a few real estate books, you will have a very good idea of what they are talking about, and you will get more out of the discussion. This is another plug to reading.

You will also meet people there who, at times, may bring deals to you for a fee. You may even find what we refer to as 'Bird Dogs' who are an excellent source for leads. These are people who will go out and look for specific deals and put them under contract and then assign them to you for a fee. You will also get to know people who you can pitch your deals to so they can partner with you when you need money. You will meet people who can do your taxes, fix the toilets, etc.

One of my favorite things to do is to find people who have expertise in areas I have an interest in and just talk to them. Most people love to share what they know as long as you respect their time. I have been able to sit down with many people to pick their brains, including expensive attorneys and the like, for the price of lunch. Some of these professionals will charge you between $100 and $200 an hour if you meet with them at their office, but will gladly talk with you for over an hour when you buy them a $12 lunch at their favorite restaurant. Remember, all you have to do is ask.

Chapter 2: KNOWING WHERE YOU STAND

Admitting Where You Are

One of the toughest books I have read is As a Man Thinketh, by James Allen. He pretty much states that people are where they are in their lives because they put themselves there through their thinking. When I first read this book, I was so disgusted because I thought it was the most ridiculous idea to think that I was broke because I put myself there. I calmed down eventually and finished reading the book, and actually liked it. I have grown a lot over the past fourteen years, and this is actually one of my favorite books and I now wholeheartedly agree with James Allen's conclusions.

Many people, like me at the beginning, blame their circumstances on everything and everybody else but themselves. If you are serious about changing your life, you need to admit that you put yourself where you are today. Once that sinks in really deep you can do something about it. Remember, you are the master of your life.

You need to determine if you want the big payout that comes from flipping houses or the slow, long term, residual income that comes from buying and holding property long term. Personally, my strategy of choice is buy and hold. If you choose the buy and hold strategy, there is a lot you have to learn to keep your projects profitable over the long haul. If you want to fix & flip, you need to seek people who are successful in that arena and learn from them.

You will also have to decide what types of properties you are looking for. If you choose the smaller multi-units, you may want to manage by yourself at the beginning to gain experience and also because it may be too expensive at hire a manager. After you have had a few properties, you can afford a manager. If you are going for smaller properties, you would want to think twice about investing 100 miles away because you have to travel to take care of maintenance. But if you specialize in bigger properties, you can afford to hire a manager from the beginning. Either way, you may want to be personally involved as much as possible to learn what is going on. You don't want someone charging you $500 for changing the faucet because you have no clue how much things cost.

Understand what is on your credit report so you can put yourself in the best light for financing. Credit reports have many erroneous data and this may keep you from getting a good interest rate or being denied financing all together. You need to review your credit report at least once every year and promptly dispute any erroneous information because it costs dearly to have bad credit.

Know your financial profile. You should be aware of how much you owe and to whom, how much the payments are, and how much money is coming in. It is a good idea to know if you have any judgments, liens, collections, and any other derogatory credit so you can start getting everything straightened out.

Most of the time, there will be money involved to close a transaction; it just does not have to come from you. If you have your own money to invest, then you don't have to bring in partners, but, for most people, that is a luxury they can't afford. You need to establish from the beginning what resources you have available to you so you can employ the right strategy for you. Fortunately, real estate investing is a game you can play with other people's money. We call this OPM, and there is an excellent book out there by the title OPM, Other People's Money by Michael A. Lechter. It is an excellent read.

Determine What You Really Want

After you admit where you are, the next step is to clearly know what you want. The best book I have read on goals and vision for your life is Think and Grow Rich, by Napoleon Hill and I would highly recommend it. Here are some characteristics that a good goal should have:

a) It must be in writing. You start owning a goal when you write it down. From personal experience, writing down a concise goal takes some thinking. You will find that, as you go through the process of writing down a goal, it becomes part of you. A lot has been written about the necessity of writing down goals and it is worth the time to read about it.

b) It must be clear and measurable. You must know exactly what you are aiming for or you will go nowhere. For example, you should aim at buying a 2-unit building by June 30th, instead of aiming at acquiring an investment property sometime.

c) Goals must have deadline. It is human nature not to be focused when we don't have deadlines. Your goals must have a deadline to get you moving, and also to help you evaluate your progress.

d) Within your control. You will have more success when you plan to pick up the phone and dial until you talk to 5 sellers/realtors per week instead of throwing an ad in the paper or internet and praying that someone will call you. Someone may call you from your ad, but that is out of your control.

e) No conflict. You will be asking for trouble if you plan to get your investing business going and also to spend more time at work. Investing requires work, and if you will succeed at it, you will need to give it the time it deserves.

f) Tell the world. Telling people about your goal puts you on the spot. Confess your goal to some loud mouths who will keep you accountable, because they will never let you live it down.

Vacancy Ratio

I like multi-unit buildings because, the more units I have, the less the vacancy factor affects me. Think through this for a minute, it does not matter what kind of property you have, you will experience vacancies from time to time. Some of the reasons for vacancies include leases running their course, tenants breaking their lease for whatever reason, some tenants just disappearing in the middle of the night without notice, etc.

It is therefore common sense that, if you have a single family home as a rental, you will experience 100% vacancy when you lose one tenant. At his point, you will have to dig into reserves or your personal savings to keep the property afloat. You will be in trouble if you can't find a renter quickly. Many single family landlords get desperate after they have sat on a vacancy for a while and rent to the first person who shows interest. They will skip screening because they have to get the thing filled.

Obviously, when you have a duplex and loose one renter, you are sitting at 50% vacancy. When you lose one tenant in a 4-plex, you have 25% vacancy and can breathe a lot easier than having 100% vacancy in a single family home. Let me continue here to make the point for multi-unit investing. If you own a 10-plex, we are talking 10% vacancy when you lose one tenant.

A 20-plex will be at 5% vacancy when you lose one tenant. You can afford to take your time to do proper screening when you have more units because you can still pay your mortgage and upkeep. As mentioned earlier, proper screening will mean less troubles in management.

Ease of Management

You will have the same management issues no matter the size of the property. It should go without saying that you will spend less time handling issues at one location than at multiple locations. Management is a hands-on job that requires you, or someone you hire, to be available 24 hours, 7 days a week, and 365 days a year. You just never know when something will go wrong, and you better be ready to swing into action or you will be in a lot of trouble.

When you have 4 single family homes as rentals in different parts of town, you will have to travel to those locations to take care of issues as they arise. This will take a lot of time, and you may find yourself with some unhappy tenants because you just can't handle their concerns in a timely manner.

When, on the other hand, you have a 4-plex, you can handle the issues of all four tenants at one stop. Your travel time is reduced substantially resulting in you having more time to do other things. When you are able to take care of problems quickly, you will have happier tenants who are more likely to stay longer. When they stay longer, you have fewer turnovers which is one of the most expensive aspects of management. Turnover is bad because you are not just left with a vacancy, you will also have the cost of fixing up the unit for the next tenant.

Consolidated Maintenance

Property maintenance will eat all your profits if not handled right. Anyone who owns property will tell you that plumbers and electricians charge between $70 and $100 dollars per hour. Some of them will charge you $60 - $70 dollars, if not more, just to come out to the property. If you call a plumber in the middle of the night because you have a blowup, you will be paying between $150 and $250 per hour. And you know what? These things happen and there is nothing you can do about it.

When you get a call from a stressed out tenant at 2:00 a.m. in the morning informing you that there is water all over the kitchen floor and they don't know where it is coming from, you will have no choice but to get it taken care of. You will either have to get out of bed to go and fix it or call someone for help. You cannot wait until morning to take care of the problem because chances are that you will have a much bigger problem, probably worth thousands of dollars of damage. If this happens at an upstairs unit, trust me, you will be hearing from the downstairs tenant too.

I don't mean to be dramatic here, but I am trying to drive the point home that maintenance is very expensive. You will have both routine and emergency maintenance that must be handled efficiently, or people will move out. When you have several units located in one building, you can have a plumber of electrician take care of multiple problems on a single visit. Remember they charge per hour, and if they have to travel to different properties located a few miles apart, you will be paying for the drive time too.

I personally like bigger properties because they generate enough income to the point where I can afford to have an on-site person who takes care of maintenance. I pay between $10 - $15 dollars an hour for their services, which is a lot cheaper than the $70 - $100 per hour charged by tradespeople. Now there are times when I have to get the expensive technicians, because the problem is beyond the capacity of the on-site maintenance person, but those times are few and far between.

Building Value

Appraisals on properties with 5 or more units are a lot different to those of 1 - 4 units. The values of smaller units are driven by the comparable sales in the vicinity. There is little you can do to increase their value when the neighboring comparables (Comps) are selling for less. Also the value of smaller properties seems to be more emotionally driven by the mood of the consumers instead of the reality of their operation.

Properties with more than 5 units are classified as commercial and therefore fall under commercial financing guidelines. Commercial financing is driven by the operation of the property. The banks lend based on the income stream the business generates. That means, if you own an apartment and manage it well (increasing income and reducing expenses), you will significantly increase its value.

The key to apartment financing is to have as high of a Net Operating Income (NOI) as possible for your property. This is the income left after you subtract all the expenses for running the building. You should note that NOI does not take into account the mortgages to be paid. The NOI is divided by Capitalization Rate (CAP Rate) to arrive at value. Simply put, CAP Rate is the ratio between the value and NOI for the area and types of property. You can get this rate from a commercial broker or appraiser in your area. There are also websites that publish this rate for different areas. See chapter 9 for more information on commercial property valuation.

Flexible Financing

There are a significantly less number of investors looking to buy small apartments as compared to 1 - 4 units. This means that owners of these small apartments will be more flexible if they want to sell their properties. These are purely the forces of supply and demand at work here. Seller financing and owner seconds are commonplace in apartment financing because the buyers are few. This spells great opportunity for the investors who can negotiate a deal that makes sense for them.

Less Competition

As mentioned in the section above, there are few buyers for small apartments. This means buyers have very little competition and can afford to take the time to put the deal together without worrying that someone else will snatch it from underneath them. I have seen properties on the market for a year or longer without anyone ever making offers. Many of these properties also go under contract and fall out of contract all the time. Sellers are therefore aware that they must be flexible with the few buyers who are interested in their properties.

Chapter 4: FINANCING

When you go to the grocery or department store, you have a very good idea of either how much cash you have in your wallet or available cash on the debit card. Meeting with a lender in advance of looking for property gives you the budget you have to work with, and this is a very good idea. Over the years, I have seen many people who go looking for and fall in love with a property only to find out they can't qualify for it. So, start developing relationships with lenders before you find the property. They can save you a lot of wasted time.

Mortgage brokers, unlike bank loan officers, work for you and they don't get paid if the loan does not close. They stake their whole existence in getting the loan for you, or they don't eat. They have relationships with several lenders, and a good loan officer will shop very hard for the best terms for you, most of the time, they work with wholesale lenders who may offer better rates than the local banks.

Mortgage brokers are paid through the loan in two ways. They get an origination fee which is normally about 1% of the loan amount. If anybody was charging more, I would shop around for a lower fee. They can also get paid what is called Yield Spread Premium (YSP) by the lender when they charge a rate higher than par. You will also hear this called "being paid in the back end." Par is the rate which the mortgage company can get from the lender without making any points or rebate. The mortgage broker can choose to charge you a higher rate, and have the lender pay them a rebate. It is up to the broker how much higher than par rate they will charge and remain competitive. Lenders will put a cap on how much higher than par the broker can charge. This can be confusing for the consumer because the broker may give some of this money back to the borrower as credit.

Banks and credit unions also do mortgage loans but have very limited loan programs available. Their underwriting guidelines are also very strict and they only tend to lend to borrowers with very high credit rating. If you have a lot of money to put down on a purchase, or have significant equity on a refinance, you may get better rates at your bank or credit union. But in most cases, a good mortgage broker will almost always beat the rates at the bank or credit union.

Credit unions customarily have very low closing costs, but their rates are higher than a mortgage broker can get for you. They just charge a higher rate and pay for the fees that a broker would have to charge. It is up to you to determine whether higher rate or fees are better for your situation. Let us get real here. Nobody works for free, and you must pay somewhere.

The following are the basics you should know about mortgages, that I call 'Mortgage 101'.

Mortgage 101

There are three main fundamentals (BIG THREE) you must understand to know how financing woks. These three, in my opinion, form the foundation of financing and knowing them will be a great starting point in discussions with your lender. It, therefore, is of paramount importance that you have a good understanding of the 'Big Three'.

1. Loan-to-Value commonly known as LTV

2. Debt-to-Income commonly known as DTI

3. Credit history as shown on the credit report

Loan-to-Value

Definition

Ratio of the amount of loan requested to the value of the property expressed as a percentage.

CLTV is combined loan-to-value ratio, and denotes that there is more than one mortgage.

LTV/CLTV requirements vary based on the following:

A. Occupancy. Owner occupied 'OO' properties will generally be granted a higher LTV than non-owner occupied 'NOO' ones. 'NOO' properties will have lower LTV and additional fees.

B. Loan purpose. Purchase money and rate-and-term 'R/T' refinance loans will allow higher LTV than cash-out 'C-O'. 'Rate and term' refinance loans are ones that do not add to the principal except for loan costs and are meant to lower the rate or the term.

C. Credit history. Credit history will determine your LTV and may cause you to be denied a loan altogether.

Why is DTI important?

1. It affects the interest rate on loans. The higher the LTV the higher the interest rate.

2. It determines the amount of Mortgage Insurance (MI/PMI) for properties with less than 20% equity for conventional loans. There are different guidelines for different loan programs.

3. It determines what loan programs a borrower is eligible for, or whether he/she qualifies for anything at all.

How to calculate DTI

1. Determine the amount of loan to apply for.

2. Establish the value of the property.

3. Divide #1/#2 and express as a percentage.

Example 1

You need a loan of $80,000 to refinance a 1st mortgage on their house that will appraise for $100,000. What is the LTV? ($80,000/$100,000) * 100 = 80%

Example 2

You need a 2nd mortgage in the amount of $25,000 for home improvement. You already have a $75,000 1st mortgage on the property that has appraised for $100,000. What is the LTV? In this case, the LTV will be called combined loan-to-value (CLTV) because there is a combination of 1st and 2nd mortgages. What is the CLTV? (($75,000 + $25,000)/ ($100,000)) * 100 = 100%

Debt-to-Income

Definition

The ratio of monthly debt obligation to gross monthly income expressed as a percentage.

Why is DTI important?

1. It determines the loan program one qualifies for.
2. It determines the loan amount one can qualify for.

How to calculate DTI

1. Determine the total monthly housing expense (PITI).
2. Determine the total of other monthly payments.

3. Determine monthly gross income.

Top Ratio = #1/#3 * 100   Bottom Ratio = ((#1 + #2) / #3) * 100

Example 1

A client works full time for ABC Company where they are paid $12.00/ hour. She wants to buy a house with a PI payment of $721, taxes of $105, and hazard insurance payments of $23 (monthly). She pays $125 in credit card payments, and $200 for a car loan. What is the top and bottom DTI?

Top DTI = ((721+105+23)/(12*40*52)/12) = 40.82%

Bottom DTI = ((721+105+23+125+200)/(12*40*52)/12) = 56.44%

DTI is communicated in a ratio of Top DTI/Bottom DTI. The example above would be written as 41/56 DTI.

Debt Service Coverage Ratio

A big factor that will come into play when you are getting a commercial loan (5+ units) is debt service coverage ratio. This is the ratio of net operating income over annual debt service. Lenders want this to be 1.2 or higher. This is very important because commercial loans are mainly based on the cash flow of the property.

Credit History

Definition

A record of the borrower's payment history for all revolving and installment debts, including public records. Understanding credit is so important that I will devote the next chapter to talking about it.

*[see copy of GFE at the end of this section]

The Good Faith Estimate (GFE):

When I was a mortgage broker, I got a lot of questions from people wanting to know what certain charges on the GFE were for (see the blank GFE included in the back of the book). For those that have never purchased real estate before, it is overwhelming to see $5,000 or more closing costs. Although they don't understand what is going on, they feel as if they are being robbed blind. Well, buying real estate is not like buying a car which only requires a few hundred dollars to consummate the deal; we are talking hundreds of thousands of dollars, so the closing costs are a magnitude out.

Lenders are required to give you a GFE three days after loan application. The GFE is designed to help the borrower understand the costs associated with buying or refinancing a property. I will painstakingly explain the charges on the GFE, line by line, to give a very clear picture of what you are looking at. Here we go:

GFE TERMS

800 ITEMS PAYABLE IN CONNECTION WITH LOAN:

801. Loan Origination: A fee charged by the loan officer for service rendered. The most common fee in the industry is 1% of the loan amount. It is up to the individual lender's policy as to how much you can move from this point.

802. Loan Discount: This is a miscellaneous entry that can stand for a variety of fees including: points to buy down a rate, adjustment fees dictated by the lender for the type and size of the loan, or to build in some extra profit for the loan officer.

803. Appraisal Fee: A fee charged by an appraiser for doing an appraisal. It is against the law to charge the borrower more than what the lender is actually billed by the appraiser. The lender may charge you upfront before an appraisal is done.

804. Credit Report: A report of the borrower's borrowing and repayment history. A credit report is mandatory for all borrowers.

805. Lender's Inspection Fee: A fee charged by the lenders for any special inspection they may require. Sometimes, an appraisal review will be required for High-LTV-Low-Doc loans.

808. Mortgage Broker Fee: Mostly profit for the Mortgage Company.

809. Tax Related Service Fee: A one-time fee paid at closing that enables notification to the lender of when and how much the taxes are to be paid by the county at each mortgage anniversary.

810. Processing Fee: A fee charged by the lender to cover for processing a loan.

811. Underwriting Fee: This fee is charged by the lender to underwrite the loan which varies depending on which lender is used.

812. Wire Transfer Fee: In this modern age, much of the world's money and information is transferred from point to point electronically. In the case of a mortgage, the lender must be able to access money from their account to fund mortgage loans all across the country. This is done by electronically transferring the amount of money that is needed for a mortgage to any closing agent. To utilize the Electronic Funds System, lenders are charged a fee each time they transfer funds. Most lenders will wire the funds to the escrow agent as one of the final steps in completing the loan process.

813. Doc Prep: A fee charged by the lender for preparing the documents that are sent to the title company for the borrower to sign at settlement.

814. Flood Cert: A mandatory fee charged by lenders to check whether the subject property is on a flood zone. Remember, they will charge this fee even if the property is located on top of a mountain with no possibility of flooding. A flood certification fee must be paid on all purchase and refinance loans.

815. Assignment Fee: The cost to record the assignment of the mortgage from the broker, banker or lender to another lender that will service the mortgage.

These last three fees (815, 816, & 817) are not printed on the GFE, but are required by every lender.

1100 TITLE CHARGES

1101. Closing and Escrow Fee: A fee charged by the title company for putting the settlement documents together, the time an escrow agent takes to explain the paperwork to a borrower at closing, and making out the checks to all the parties in a transaction.

1105. Document Preparation Fee: A fee a title company may charge for the time they take to put the paperwork in the right format for the borrower to sign at closing.

1106.   Notary Fee: A fee charged by the title company for any additional paperwork they have to do which requires the signature of a notary public.

1107.   Attorney Fees: Any additional work the title company has to do in a legal capacity or any other attorney fees in relation to the transaction.

1108.   Title Insurance: A fee charged by the title insurance company to cover for the   protection of a borrower in case of any defects in the title policy they offer.

1109.   Endorsements: Title Insurance coverage on specific items required by the lender. The most common are:

*Form 100 (Comprehensive Lender's Endorsement): Comprehensive coverage for the lender insuring against violation of covenants, encroachments of the main dwelling and association liens affecting priority of the loan.

*Form 8.1 (Environmental Protection): Coverage ensuring that no environmental lien has been filed either in the clerk and recorder's records or filed in the U.S. District Court.

1110.   Courier/FedEx: Fee charged by the title company to overnight payoff checks to lenders who will be paid in the refinance.

1200 GOVERNMENT RECORDING & TRANSFER CHARGES:

1201. Recording Fee. A fee paid by the title company to record the trust deed at the   county recorder's office.

1202.   City/County Tax/Stamp: We have never encountered this in loans we have done.

1203.   State Tax/Stamps: Same as 1202.

1300 ADDITIONAL SETTLEMENT CHARGES:

1302: Pest Inspection: A fee charged by pest Inspection Company for their work.

Estimated Closing Costs: A total of sections 800, 1100, 1200, & 1300.

900 ITEMS REQUIRED BY LENDER TO BE PAID IN ADVANCE:

901.   Interest for: The number of days from the funding date to the 1st of the following month.

902.   Mortgage Insurance Premium: Any mortgage insurance amount the lender requires.

903.   Hazard Insurance Premium: Home owners insurance premium required by lender. This amount depends on how the policy for the subject property is written. It is always a full year of homeowners insurance on purchase loans.

905.   VA Funding Fee: A one-time fee required by the Veteran Administration on VA loans.

1000 RESERVES DEPOSITED WITH LENDER:

1001.   Hazard Insurance Premiums: Usually 2 months' worth of hazard insurance that the lender requires as a cushion to make sure there are enough reserves in escrow to cover any insurance increases.

1002.   Mortgage Ins. Premium Reserves: Usually 2 months' worth of mortgage insurance   to cover any insurance cost increases.

1003.   School Tax: A tax that may by charged in some areas for schools.

1004.   Taxes and Assessment Reserves: An amount to pay the taxes for the year the property is purchased or refinanced.

1005. Flood Insurance Reserves: Charged on the properties that require flood insurance.

Estimated Prepaid Reserves: The total of sections 900 and 1000.

TOTAL ESTIMATED SETTLEMENT CHARGES: Total of all fees mentioned above.

COMPENSATION TO BROKER: This section is usually left blank.

TOTAL ESTIMATED FUNDS NEEDED TO CLOSE:

Purchase Price/Payoff (+): The amount of the purchase or refinance loan.

Loan Amount (-): The amount of the new loan.

Estimated Closing Costs (+): Total of sections 800, 1100, 1200, & 1300.

Est. Prepaid Items/Reserve (+): Total of sections 900 and 1000.

Amount Paid by Seller (-): Amount of closing costs to be paid by seller.

New First Mortgage (-): 1st mortgage in a situation where the loan has to be taken out in two loans.

Sub Financing (-): New 2nd mortgage.

New 2nd Mtg. Closing Costs (+): Closing costs associated with 2nd mortgage.

Total Est. Funds needed to close: The amount of money borrower will get at closing. If there are parentheses around the amount – as in ($XXX) – the borrower will need to come up with the amount shown.

GOOD FAITH ESTIMATE

Applicants:
Property Addr:
Prepared By:

Application No:
Date Prepared: 01/01/20XX
Loan Program:

The information provided below reflects estimates of the charges which you are likely to incur at the settlement of your loan. The fees listed are estimates-actual charges may be more or less. Your transaction may not involve a fee for every item listed. The numbers listed beside the estimates generally correspond to the numbered lines contained in the HUD-1 settlement statement which you will be receiving at settlement. The HUD-1 settlement statement will show you the actual cost for items paid at settlement.

Total Loan Amount $ Interest Rate: %   Term: mths

800	ITEMS PAYABLE IN CONNECTION WITH LOAN:		PFC S F POC
801	Loan Origination Fee	$	
802	Loan Discount		
803	Appraisal Fee		
804	Credit Report		
805	Lender's Inspection Fee		
808	Mortgage Broker Fee		
809	Tax Related Service Fee		
810	Processing Fee		
811	Underwriting Fee		
812	Wire Transfer Fee		
1100	TITLE CHARGES:		PFC S F POC
1101	Closing or Escrow Fee:	$	
1105	Document Preparation Fee		
1106	Notary Fees		
1107	Attorney Fees		
1108	Title Insurance:		
1200	GOVERNMENT RECORDING & TRANSFER CHARGES:		PFC S F POC
1201	Recording Fees:	$	
1202	City/County Tax/Stamps:		
1203	State Tax/Stamps:		
1300	ADDITIONAL SETTLEMENT CHARGES:		PFC S F POC
1302	Pest Inspection	$	
900	ITEMS REQUIRED BY LENDER TO BE PAID IN ADVANCE:		PFC S F POC
901	Interest for days @ $ per day	$	
902	Mortgage Insurance Premium		
903	Hazard Insurance Premium		
904			
905	VA Funding Fee		
1000	RESERVES DEPOSITED WITH LENDER:		PFC S F POC
1001	Hazard Insurance Premiums months @ $ per month	$	
1002	Mortgage Ins. Premium Reserves months @ $ per month		
1003	School Tax months @ $ per month		
1004	Taxes and Assessment Reserves months @ $ per month		
1005	Flood Insurance Reserves months @ $ per month		
	months @ $ per month		
	months @ $ per month		

Estimated Prepaid Items/Reserves

TOTAL ESTIMATED SETTLEMENT CHARGES

TOTAL ESTIMATED FUNDS NEEDED TO CLOSE: PAYMENT:		TOTAL ESTIMATED MONTHLY
Purchase Price/Payoff (+)	New First Mortgage(-)	Principal & Interest
Loan Amount (-)	Sub Financing(-)	Other Financing (P & I)
Est. Closing Costs (+)	New 2nd Mtg Closing Costs(+)	Hazard Insurance
Est. Prepaid Items/Reserves (+)		Real Estate Taxes
Amount Paid by Seller (-)		Mortgage Insurance
		Homeowner Assn. Dues
		Other
Total Est. Funds to close		**Total Monthly Payment**

These estimates are provided pursuant to the Real Estate Settlement Procedures Act of 1974, as amended (RESPA). Additional information can be found in the HUD Special Information Booklet, which is to be provided to you by your mortgage broker or lender, if your application is to purchase residential real property and the lender will take a first lien on the property.   The undersigned acknowledges receipt of the booklet "Settlement Costs," and if applicable the Consumer Handbook on ARM Mortgages.

Applicant   Date   Applicant   Date

27 ~ Real Estate Investing

Chapter 5: UNDERSTANDING CREDIT

Probably one of the most important things anyone can do financially is to build and maintain a clean credit history. In lending, a good credit rating makes the difference between a conforming/conventional, lower interest rate loan and a non-conforming loan with a higher interest rate and less favorable terms. Some individuals have let their credit go into such disarray that it prevents them from present credit purchases. The credit report is very important now that we are a society that depends on information to function. The credit report can say a lot about an individual and their personal habits and modes of operation. Just like Santa Claus, keeping track of who is naughty and nice, the credit report keeps track of our spending and repayment histories as well, and some of them are not so nice. In this section, we will cover the importance of credit and how to read and understand the credit report and all of its many aspects.

The lenders needs to understand the degree of risk they are taking in lending to a stranger a large sum of money for a long period of time. Due to this fact, the credit report will show the lender critical information, and will aid the lender in establishing if the loan candidate should have their lending request granted. Information listed on a credit report includes: Payment in good Standing, Late Payments, Collections, Liens, Judgments & Bankruptcies. As a borrower, you have the right to challenge any derogatory information on a credit report but it is up to you to prove the information is incorrect. Most of the negative information reported will remain on the credit report for seven or ten years. Bankruptcies can still show on the credit report for a period up to ten years from the time of discharge. The credit report is the lenders' main yardstick to evaluate the amount of risk that you pose.

When evaluating the credit report it is important to review the historical status of the report. This refers to the payment history of the borrower(s). The following is an explanation of terms lenders use to describe a negative credit profile:

1. *TIMES PAST DUE:* The fact that someone has some past due entries does not in itself disqualify him from qualifying for a loan, but the entries may require explanation. If your credit profile shows that you have been PAST DUE many times, you will be in trouble. You should double check though to make sure that the creditor is reporting accurately. I have seen instances where someone pays a bill after the due date and the creditor does not process it until the following month. The creditor then reports the payment as being 30 days late. You should fight reporting like this

because you were technically not 30 days late. It is their problem and not yours that they did not process it when it was received. Don't let their credit departments intimidate you on this one, because they have no legal basis for doing this.

2. *LATE PAYMENTS:* The most significant problems are those where the late payments have occurred within the last twelve months. Some lenders, however, are concerned about any late payments occurring within the previous two years. If the late payments are due to a major one-time event such as medical or disability and can be verified, the underwriter will give that kind of reason more credence than a statement that the bill got misplaced.

3. *COLLECTION:* This is trouble, especially if there are a lot of them.

4. *PAID COLLECTIONS*: These are better than open collections.

5. *CHARGE OFF:* This means that a creditor got tired of trying to collect a debt and wrote it off as a loss.

6. *120 DAYS DELINQUENT:* This is very bad. It must be resolved, because lenders will have a hard time lending to a borrower who refuses to pay a debt.

7. *INQUIRIES:* At the end of the credit report you will find a section that indicates how many inquiries have been made recently into your credit status. Are you shopping for mortgage loans? Are you incurring additional debt? Have you been turned down by others for credit? Do several inquiries indicate that you cannot qualify for a loan? These are the types of questions that you are creating in the underwriter's mind when they see multiple inquiries.

8. *JUDGEMENT/LIEN:* These must be paid before a loan is acquired or be paid off as part of a refinance.

When a negative entry appears on the credit report, it does not always mean the loan is dead. Lenders are willing to accept some blemishes and will still grant the loan. Lenders are willing to work with you provided you make an honest effort to correct existing problems.

There are obviously going to be occasions where you cannot get past the credit report. It is best to discover quickly whether there are major problems with your credit so that you can get them fixed to give yourself a better chance.

Why are there uncertainties in closing costs?

    a. Lenders may not be able to set a firm closing date at the beginning of the loan process. Therefore, the number of days to collect interest for is unclear.

    b. They may not know the actual hazard insurance premium, especially if the loan amount is changing. This will change the amount of monthly payments and also the amount of reserves.

    c. The actual existing mortgage payoff may not be known until you get it in writing from the mortgage company. The loan amount may need adjusting to make sure that the new loan is sufficient to cover the outstanding loan including any closing costs.

    d. At loan application, the lender might not know the actual amount of property taxes. Taxes go up from time to time. An estimate has to be done based on previous years' taxes.

Cleaning your credit profile

If your credit report has blemishes, do not despair. You must, however, understand that it will take time to get it cleaned. The way to start is to get a free credit report from www.annualcreditreport.com and scrutinize it to find if there is information that is inaccurate. This is a website that was mandated by Congress a few years ago to give the consumer a way to keep tabs on their credit profile. You are entitled to one free report every twelve months, if you want it more often than that, you will have to pay. When you log onto the website, there will be personal information that only you will know. After you get past the screening, you will be able to log into the individual credit bureaus to request a report. The major bureaus are Experian, Equifax, and Transunion.

When you pull the report, make sure to write down the login, password, and file number so you are able to login in the future to view your report and, most importantly, to dispute any inaccurate information. You can dispute entries right on the site and the bureaus must investigate and give you an update within 45 to 60 days. If they cannot find the creditor to validate the entries, they must remove them and notify you of the action.

The reports you get from this system will not show a credit score, but it is an excellent free way to get going on cleaning your credit. It is important that you start this process early in the loan process because 60 days feels like eternity when you are trying to lock a certain rate.

If you must get the errors removed right away so you can qualify for a loan, you can contact your lender to do what we call a 'rapid rescore' which will take about 3 to 5 days to complete. This process requires letters from creditors confirming the status of the debt. The scores are updated after the process and, based on the updates made; you may see a big jump in your scores. One thing to bear in mind is that rapid rescore is not cheap. It will cost you anywhere from $30 to $50 per account (tradeline) per credit bureau.

There is really no easy way of getting rid of bad credit from your profile if it is accurately reported. Here is an example I have used in the past to explain to my clients how it works:

When you have sugar or salt water, the only way to reduce the effect is by diluting it by adding fresh water (of course we are ignoring distillation and other scientific methods). As you add fresh water, the salt or sugar flavor goes away until there comes a time when you can't tell that the water wasn't fresh. Credit works a lot in the same way. Once you have problems, the sure way to rectify them is as follows:

a) Contact the creditors and work out payment arrangements if possible

b) Payoff or settle collections, judgments, and liens

c) Pay your bills on time

d) Get new credit lines and never be late

As you do this, the effect of the bad credit is reduced and the good credit overshadows the bad. With persistence, the scores will get high enough to where you can get financing.

Are credit repair companies worth it?

It is my opinion that most = credit repair companies are a rip off. First off they are very expensive and there really is nothing they can do for you that you can't do for yourself. If, however, you don't have the time to follow up with all the disputes, you may want to pay them to do it. What is interesting is that they cannot charge you for repairing your credit, so they sell you some bogus book or some program to justify charging you hundreds or thousands of dollars. There are a few good companies out there that will charge you only after they produce results. Once again, you should do your research before you part with your money.

Chapter 6: IT IS A TEAM SPORT

Real estate investing is a team sport because there are many aspects that require different skills that you just can't possess all by yourself. You will need Realtors, Title Companies, Appraisers, General Contractors, Lawyers, Accountants, etc., to be successful. You will coordinate the activities of all these professionals and take their input, but, at the end of the day, you must make the ultimate decision to buy or to pass on deals. You are like the quarter back of your team.

Realtors

Realtors work for whoever hired them. If you as a buyer are dealing with a realtor who has a listing, they work for the seller not you. For example, when you go to an open house, the realtor you meet there is working exclusively for the seller and you better be careful what information you divulge to them. Also, when you call a realtor from an ad about a specific property you are interested in seeing, you should know that they are working for the seller who hired them.

The seller generally pays the commission on a transaction. When your realtor, contacts the listing realtor, and shows you properties, they both get paid by the seller. The commission is already built into the listing price to take care of the realtors. The only time you may have to pay the agent is if you buy a 'For Sale By Owner' property (FSBO) whereby the agent is not able to have the seller agree to pay a commission.

It is my opinion that you should always get your own agent to represent your interest because, after all, the seller pays them. Realtors are like attorneys in that they are discreet with information and can use anything you say against you in a negotiation. For example, if you go to an open house without your realtor and divulge to the listing agent that you love the house and can pay the full asking price, you shouldn't be shocked when the seller insists on getting the full listing price. On the other hand, you can tell this information to your agent, and, if they are good, they should still help you get the lowest price possible. Be careful, if they are dishonest, they may push you to pay the higher price because their commission would be higher. Personally, I don't trust anybody, and will not tell them that information, because it is nobody's business.

You must bear in mind that people are motivated by personal interest, period. Realtors are no different, especially because the commissions involved are really big. Remember that, if you make a bad purchase because of anybody's advice, you are the one who will be stuck paying for it. You should interview several realtors and choose the one who you get along with the best. The best way I have found is to ask friends and family who they have worked with in the past that they liked. Also, ask your title company to make a recommendation. They work with many realtors on a daily basis, and know the good ones. They may not give you a list for fear of getting sued, but when you ask them about ones you are considering, they will tell you who to steer away from. Once again, I would like to reiterate that I ask for advice from many people, but take what they say with a grain of salt. Now, after you have worked with somebody on a few deals and they have taken good care of you, you can start trusting their advice. Just remember, if things go bad, you are the only one who will be left holding the bag.

Appraiser

Appraisers, like realtors and mortgage professionals are regulated by the Division of Real Estate or other government agency. When you are getting institutional lender financing, an appraisal is required. Nowadays, the lenders request the appraisal, so the investor cannot easily influence them.

If you have a good relationship with appraisers, you can have them check out properties you are considering buying and give you an opinion of value. This can be a great time saving device. They can also take the time to educate you on what repairs produce most increase in property value. This is invaluable in that you learn how to spend the least amount of money to get most value, or, as they say, the biggest bang for your buck.

There are different appraisal methods for different types of properties. Single family properties lean towards the market approach method which compares the subject property to similar properties in the vicinity that have recently sold. 2 – 4 units use a combination of comparable and rent multiplier analysis. In other words, the appraiser looks closely at the rents the property is bringing in and justifies it with rents of other like properties sold.

5+ units fall under the category of commercial properties and are appraised mainly based on the income stream they generate. Please see Chapter 8 for more details on this.

Points to note on 1 – 4 units

1. In most cases, rental properties will require a rental analysis in addition to the appraisal. This is required when a high rental income is used to qualify. The additional analysis costs money.

2. If a rental property has multiple units that are rented by different tenants, the property will have to be zoned for multi-unit to count the rents as qualifying income.

3. You will not be allowed to use rent from a mother-in-law apartment if the area is not zoned for such property. There may be exceptions when doing loan modifications.

4. All qualifying rental income must be claimed on taxes. If the borrower just pockets the rent, it will not be counted.

5. A rental agreement is required on all rentals to count the income towards qualifying.

Title Companies

Title companies search property records to determine the true ownership, whether there are any liens against the property, and possibly determine if the title is clouded in any way. After the title company searches the records and determines that the property has no liens, judgments, or anything else forbidding clear title, a Title Insurance policy is issued. This insurance provides protection against errors in the transfer of title to the new owner and ensures that the seller gets paid for their interest in the property.

It is at the title company that the settlement statement, or 'HUD-1', is put together, which is the document showing the final numbers to be paid to complete the transaction. The title company will also assemble the final documents necessary for completing the sale, obtain the necessary signatures of the concerned parties, and record the transaction.

Many title companies provide other great services. Of course, as with anything else, you need to have a good working relationship with them. When I am considering purchasing a property, I can call my title company and, within minutes, they will tell me how much was paid for the property, when it was purchased, the name of the lender, and if there are liens on the title. They can also tell me if the owner is behind on taxes, if there is more than one owner, etc.

This is great information to know when I am talking to a seller because they will not just feed me lies because I know a lot about their property.

I have also used them to prepare Quit Claim Deeds when I need to transfer ownership of property for a legitimate reason. Title companies are a wealth of information and, if you develop a relationship with them, they are loyal, they will act like your back office feeding you all the good information. They can give you lists of properties with seller contact information based on several categories you may need for marketing.

Points worth noting

1. If there are any judgments or liens appearing on the title, they will have to be cleared before the loan can close. They should either be paid up front, or paid as part of a refinance with lender permission. The lender may also require them to be paid before the loan can close.

2. If a borrower wants to do the loan in their name alone and then add their spouse or someone else on the title later on, they will need to sign a Quit Claim Deed to accomplish that. It is best they all come to the closing together so that they can sign all the paperwork at the same time.

General Contractors

General contractors see things an average buyer can't see. They can walk through the property with you and point out all sorts of structural problems that would easily escape your untrained eye. They also seem to know just the correct questions to ask the owners. I have been able to get this service for the price of lunch, but it is worth paying an hourly consulting fee if you have to.

Property Manager

Property managers are a wealth of information about how to do things right. I have personally managed my own properties and have learned a lot over the years about what works and what does not. Here is a way that you can get help from your local property manager. Just call them up and state that you are buying an investment property and are not sure if you will manage it by yourself or hire a manager. Ask them to come check it out with you and tell you what it would take to run the place. You will get cooperation because the manager is hoping you will hire them to manage the property. Ask them questions like, "How would you reduce costs and increase income on the property?"

Accountant

Please consult with your accountant on the tax consequences of buying the property you are considering. They will also advise you on how to run your business in the most efficient manner possible to get maximum tax benefits.

Lawyer

Lawyers will advise you on the best business structures to use and how to stay out of jail. They tend to be very expensive, but, as with anybody else, I can get an hour of advice for the price of lunch. I find that I need legal advice more in dealing with tenants, and there are programs out there that you can sign up for where you have unlimited access to an attorney for a nominal fee.

Chapter 7: PROPERTY AND LOCATION

Finding the Property

There are different ways to find deals ranging from realtors to the internet, newspapers, walking the neighborhoods, networking, and others. When you deal in multi-units, there are plenty of deals on the market to choose from. Unlike fix & flips deals, for which you have to network like crazy and jump on deals because of stiff competition, multi-family deals are plentiful and take a long time to sell because many investors are scared to go after them.

I find that there are more investors who go after single family properties and fewer go after bigger properties. Most investors will not attempt anything bigger than 3-unit building, and even fewer will go for anything bigger than 4 units. This results in a lot less competition and you can take your time picking out the deals and negotiating for the terms you can live with.

Because many investors don't go after these properties, you can find many flexible sellers who will sell on terms to make the properties move. This is exactly why I focus on these properties, because I like taking my time to make sure that I am making a wise investment decision.

You can get multi-unit listings from your realtor or search the public version of the Multiple Listing Service (MLS) available in many areas which is tied to the MLS used by realtors. Once you find the properties you want, you can just give your realtor the MLS numbers and they can get you more information. You can also find income property listing in your local newspaper and other real estate print. One of the most excellent sources for multi-unit listings is www.loopnet.com.

In my opinion, there are many deals to go after, but most people just don't have the guts to go after them. There are properties out there that have been on the market for over six months and never had anybody make offers. Most investors just shy away after they see the asking price, because they assume that the seller is not negotiable.

The most important decision in going after the deal is the location. If I like the location, I contact the realtor or seller and request for financials and make the offer. I make my offer based on the financials and do not care what the asking price is. Obviously, I am told "NO" most of the time, but once in a while I will find someone reasonable who wants to work with me.

Location, Location, Location

As I have mentioned above, the first criteria for choosing investment property for holding long term should be location. I pick locations based on supply and demand forces. For example, I like properties located in college towns because there is a built in supply of tenants and the demand is there. If you go after college towns, you should be aware that you may experience massive vacancies during the summer months.

It can be disastrous to pick a city that has an economy that is not diversified. If the employer is a single industry, you may get in trouble if that industry collapses. A friend of mine tried to get me to partner with him on some property in Vernal, Utah, when the gas industry was booming. Studio apartments were renting for over $1000 and the returns were significant. I have heard that there were over 30,000 jobs virtually overnight, and housing was scarce. I told my friend that I was not comfortable with that strategy because the economy in Vernal was reliant on a single industry. A few months later, there was a shift in the laws and gas exploration was practically shut down. About 25,000 people had to be let go, and I bet the vacancy rate is quite high in Vernal now. I am glad that I was not suckered into investing there.

Of course, you want to choose properties with great freeway access and close to services like restaurants and shopping. I always check with the city zoning and planning departments to find out what is in the works for the areas I am considering. You may buy a property with a major road scheduled to go through the backyard. This of course would ruin your investment. Remember, city officials work for you and you should not hesitate in talking to them. I am old school and prefer face-to-face meetings with them. I think I get more input when I take time to make an appointment and drive to their office to meet with them.

I also make it a point to walk the area and talk to the neighbors about the building and to get general information that may be helpful. On one memorable occasion, I got a 4-plex under contract in Logan, Utah, because it was an exceptional value. It is within walking distance to services, and I thought that I had found a great deal. On talking to the neighbors about the property, I found that the city had decided to reclaim the park strips that had over the years been converted to parking spaces by investors. This was a big problem because the only parking for the building was in the front of the 4-plex, and if the city wouldn't allow parking there, there would be no parking whatsoever. I talked to the planning department of the city and they confirmed what the neighbors had told me and even provided the minutes of the meeting at which the decision to take back the parking strip was passed. This was great information and I used it to get out of the contract for non-disclosure of material fact.

Police departments will give you all sorts of crime statistics for your area of interest just for the asking. In one small town, the chief of police went ahead to show me how many times officers had been called to this one apartment complex we were considering. He even divulged what kinds of incidents had occurred, and how many arrests had been made in a 12 month period. Of course, not every police department will be this friendly, but most of them are very helpful. Police departments want to have good neighborhoods because they get called out less frequently. They love investors who make an effort to keep crime out because that is one less thing they have to worry about.

Chapter 8: IS IT A DIAMOND OR A LEMON?

This is where the rubber meets the road. No management can fix a property that you paid too much for. You can do everything right, but if you pay too much, you are in trouble. It is of paramount importance that you thoroughly understand the steps you ought to follow to analyze a deal.

Remember, good things are simple. If you don't understand the investment, get some help before proceeding, or don't do it. Robert T. Kiyosaki has a great definition for good and bad deals that is very simple to understand:

A good deal puts money in your pocket

A bad deal takes money out of your pocket

It is really that simple. Don't complicate or over analyze things. If the numbers add up, make the next move; if they don't, walk away. If you find you are trying to convince yourself, then you really don't have a deal. I buy property based on the present financial picture and never on the future. I really don't know what will happen in the future and neither do your realtor and definitely not the seller. I want to buy based on today's numbers, and any improvements I make are a bonus for me and my partners.

Here are the steps:

STEP 1: DETERMINE GROSS OPERATING INCOME (GOI)

1. Determine Income:

In multi-family properties, there are mainly two sources of income. You must have an accurate accounting of income since this is the money you will be using to pay for the expenses and the mortgage, and hopefully have some leftover. The two sources of income are discussed below:

i)   Rental income. This is the money that comes from rents that tenants pay every month. Be sure to verify that the numbers you are receiving are what actually is received, not hypothetical ones. Most listings represent the 'Gross Scheduled Rental Income' as the income generated by a property. This is actually what the property would generate if it was 100% occupied. Upon a few minutes of prodding, you will also find that this is mainly what the rents would be if all units were rented at market rates. If you use this number as a basis for your calculation, you are in trouble because they are just fictional, and not what the property is actually generating.

ii)   Other income. This is money generated from laundry machines, vending, etc. This, again, can be inflated. I like to see actual financials for the past 3 years to verify any information I receive from seller or realtor.

Example

You drive by a 5-plex that is listed for $380,000 and take a flier that has the following information:

Number of Apts	Bed Rms	Bth Rms	Approx Sq	Rent
4	2	1	600	625
1	1	1	500	500

Gross Sched. Inc: $36,000   # Electric Meters: 5   # Gas Meters: 5

THEORY

The gross rents for the property will be $36,000 per year .

REALITY CHECK

You request the actual numbers and the realtor provides the following information from sellers:

November rents:
Unit #1: $580   Unit #4: $590
Unit #2: $625   Unit #5: $600
Unit #3: $500

Annual expenses: Other information:
Taxes: $2,300   Tenants pay power & gas
Insurance: $500   Sellers manage property
Maintenance: $2,400
Water & Sewer: $1,800

This means that the actual income (based on November rents) is $34,740, not $36,000. Had you bought without verifying the rents, you would have $1,260 less income than you planned.

The best way to determine the income and expenses with no guesswork involved is to get the seller's Schedule 'E' of tax returns. But let us say that it is too early in the game and you will get that later.

2. **Determine Vacancy Rate:**

You can get the vacancy rate from the seller, or realtor. You will be lucky to find a seller who will give you accurate figure, but you can use their number as a start. Don't buy the line that the property is always 100%, because every property has a vacancy component. A vacancy may result from tenants leaving, abandoning the property, or by the necessary time it will take to fix up a property after tenants leave at the end of the lease. It really does not matter how the vacancy is created, it will cost you money.

You may get this number from a local property manager, or from owners of neighboring properties. Property management companies are a wealth of information if you know how to handle them correctly.

Remember that the bank will at best use 5 - 7% in determining the loan to extend to you even if the property is 100% occupied at the moment. You should make it a point to use the vacancy rate used by the bank or higher because, even though you may be getting seller financing to purchase the property, the banks are likely to be obtained in refinancing down the road.

THEORY

The realtor tells you that the property is 100% occupied and, whenever there is vacancy, it gets filled within 1 week. They just stick a sign on the front lawn and that does the job.

REALITY CHECK

You check with a property manager who knows the area well and he states that the vacancy rate is 6% of gross schedule rents.

You would also be wise to expect to spend some money on advertising. When you have a vacancy for two weeks, you will probably be motivated to look at other avenues to get the vacancy filled.

Gross Operating Income for your property will be:

Income: $34,740

Vacancy: $34,740 x 6% = $2,084.40

GOI: $34,740 - $2,080.40 = $32,655.60

Income – Vacancy = Gross Operating Income

STEP 2: DETERMINE OPERATING EXPENSES

After you determine the actual income you have to work with, you will want to turn your attention to the expenses. Most people underestimate how expensive it is to run a property. As you will see from the list below, there are many expenses, some of which are not that easy to pinpoint accurately. In my experience, expenses for running a small multi-family property will average between 30% - 45% or higher depending on who is responsible to pay what utilities. This is not an exhaustive list, but it will give you a good idea of what to expect. Some properties may not have all the items listed here, and others may have more. Work with your team to identify all the expenses that are associated with the property you are purchasing. Here is the list:

iii) Accounting & legal. Most investors own property under a legal entity to protect their other assets in case of a lawsuit. The legal entities have separate tax returns which will cost you and may have other legal expenses associated with them.

iv) Advertising, Licensing & Permits. Depending on what kind of advertising you have to do to keep the property occupied, the expense can be a few hundred to a few thousand per year. Also different municipalities have different kinds of licensing and permit fees you must pay to operate a rental. Check with them for what is required.

v) Property Insurance. Insurance is one of the biggest expenses in property ownership but you can't afford not to have it. Moreover, if you get bank financing, they will require that you have insurance and determine the amount of coverage. If you have personal property like snow removal equipment, expensive maintenance equipment, etc., it may be a good idea to have insurance to cover those items. Talk to your trusted insurance agent about what you need.

vi) Property Management. Call some property management companies to find out how much they charge to manage a property of the size you are planning to buy. They will gladly give this information to you if you handle them tactfully. If you plan to manage by yourself, you should still pay yourself because your time is worth something. After all, this is a business you are running.

vii) Property Taxes. Property taxes are easy to pinpoint accurately. All you have to do is call the county Recorder's Office and they will give this information to you. Your title company can also give this information to you fairly quickly.

viii) Repair & Maintenance. Maintenance is expensive and must be done in a timely manner if you want to keep your tenants. Sellers will always understate the maintenance, but you can verify their numbers using what they reported on Schedule 'E' of their tax return. Make sure to understand how snow removal is handled because this can be a very expensive item.

ix) Office supplies. This includes the photocopies, mailing, faxing, phone expenses, etc. If you don't have enough information to establish this number, you may want to use 1% of the gross operating income.

x) Utilities. These are very easy to determine. Get the account numbers from the seller and call the utility companies and explain that you are in the process of purchasing the property. They will give you the information, including the high and low usage data. You may want to work out an equal payment plan for gas and electricity for ease of budgeting. If a utility company will not disclose this information, you will need to get the seller to call them and authorize you to get the information. The utilities include the following:

a) Electricity
b) Gas & Oil
c) Sewer
d) Garbage
e) Water

xi) Miscellaneous/Replacement Reserve. It is smart to have a miscellaneous expense for items that you underestimate or leave out altogether. There are many unknowns when you are purchasing income property and you want to minimize the effect by building in a miscellaneous reserve. You will also want to have a replacement reserve which you will use to fix big ticket items like water heaters, roofs, etc. A rule of thumb I have seen many people use is 1 month's rental income.

THEORY

The expenses disclosed by the seller are: Taxes: $2300, Insurance: $500, Maintenance: $2400,

Water & Sewer: $1800. These add up to $7,000.

REALITY CHECK

At the least, there are expenses for advertising and management that you should be concerned about and you will definitely want to have a reserve for the unexpected. Let us assume for now that those are the only items to consider.

Again, you check with your local property management company and they tell you that you ought to estimate at least 1% of GOI for advertising and 10% for management. They also advise you to have a reserve of at least $200/unit.

Operating Expenses will be:

Advertising: $34,740 x 1% = $347.40

Management: $34,740 x 10% = $3,474

Reserve: 5 units x $200 = $1,000

Water & Sewer: $1,800

Taxes: $2,300

Insurance: $500

Maintenance: $2,400

Total Operating Expenses:
$347.40 + $3,474 + $1,000 + $2,300 + $500 + $2,400 + $1,800 = $11,821.40

Had you just used the expenses number given by the sellers of $7,000, you would be $4,821.40 ($11,821.40 - $7,000) in the red.

STEP 3: DETERMINE NET OPERATING INCOME (NOI)

To determine the NOI, simply subtract the operating expenses from the gross operating income. This is the money you have left after the expenses to pay the mortgage and hopefully have some left over for profit.

THEORY

If you used the seller's numbers without verifying, here is what your NOI would look like:

GOI = $36,000 (Step 1)
Expenses: $7,000 (Step 2)

NOI: $36,000 - $7,000 = $29,000

REALITY CHECK

By using the numbers you received from the realtor and your local property manager, here is how the NOI looks now:
GOI = $34,740 (Step 1)
Expenses: $11,821.40 (Step 2)
NOI: $32,655.60 - $11,821.40 = $20,821.20

This is a $8,178.80 difference, which, as you will see later, has a tremendous effect on the value of the property.

STEP 1 - STEP 2 = Net Operating Income (NOI)

STEP 4: DETERMINE CAPITALIZATION RATE

CAP rate is the ratio of net operating income to value. This ratio is expressed as a percentage and it is area and property type specific. Typical CAP rates range from 6% to 10%, but remember, they vary depending on property type and area.

You can get it from a broker or commercial appraiser. The higher the CAP rate the lower the property value, and the reverse is true. Many people leave out many of the expenses discussed above to show a higher CAP Rate. The idea is that many buyers assume that properties with a high CAP rate are a good value, but you really need to get to the bottom of the financials to determine if you have a good deal or a stinker.

The listing realtor may or may not give you the CAP rate for the area, but you can find this very easily by calling a commercial realtor or appraiser familiar with the area. Let us assume that you make such a call and find out that the CAP rate is 7.5%.

STEP 5: DETERMINE PROPERTY VALUE

Value is calculated by dividing net operating income by the CAP rate.

THEORY

Based on the numbers shown in the listing, the property value should be $29,000 / 7.5% = $386,666, or approximately $386,700.

Based on the numbers we got from the realtors and property manager, the property value is $277,289.33, or approximately $278,000. You get this by dividing $20,821.20 by 7.5%. This is over $108,000 difference in value because we verifi ed some numbers.

Remember what the listing price was? It was $380,000. Now, be honest. Did that look like a reasonable price for a 5-plex? I hope that you have seen how small variations in numbers can have big impact on final value.

STEP 3 / STEP 4 = VALUE

STEP 6: DETERMINE CASH FLOW BEFORE TAXES (CFBT)

Personally, I don't care much about STEPS 4 & 5, because I buy based on CFBT. I raise the down payment required to buy the property from investors and pay them a high return on their investment, or give them an ownership interest in the property. Because I have to pay back investors high interest rates, I only buy properties that have a healthy cash flow to be in business.

Cash flow before taxes is determined by subtracting the annual debt service (mortgage payments) from the NOI. If, after you do the subtraction, you have a negative or a very low number, you may want to rethink what you are doing. Let us assume that you have talked to a lender who states that you can get an 80% LTV loan at 7% interest. The term of the loan will be 25 years. Term means the number of years the loan is amortized over.

THEORY

If you buy the property at the listing price, and assume that the income is $36,000 and expenses are $7,000 (without taking into account the cost of advertising, management, and reserve) your monthly payment will be $2,148.61—or $25,783.32 annually. Remember, the NOI in this scenario was $29,000; therefore, the CFBT is $3,216.68.

REALITY CHECK

If you buy at the listing price because it looks like a good deal, you will be in trouble. Remember, the GOI is $32,655.60 and the expenses are $11,821.40, resulting in an NOI of $20,821.20. The mortgage payments add up to $25,783.32.

Do you see a problem here? The mortgage payment is higher than the available income after you pay for the operation of the property. You will be $4,962.12 ($20,821.20 – $25,783.32) in the negative already. You put down $76,000 to buy the property and are in seriously negative territory. This, my friend, is what we call an alligator; an animal that eats you whole.

STEP 3 – Annual Debt Service = CFBT

Chapter 9: GETTING OVER YOUR FEAR

Now that you have your mindset right, understand financing and credit, have built your team, identified the right locations, and theoretically know how to analyze a deal, it is time to get to the real stuff. You are probably itching to start working on some deals and see how it all comes together.

Ask the right questions

Once you know what you are looking for, the next step is having a list of viable properties and blocking the time out to make the calls. I like to sit down and call several sellers and/or realtors at a time. Be prepared to leave a message in case they are not available. All you need to say is something like, "Hello, my name is <u>your name</u> and I am calling about the property located at <u>XYZ Street</u>. I was wondering if it is still available and would like to find out more information about it. Please call me at 210-111-2222."

When they call back and say it is available, I get down to my list of questions. Usually when they call you back they will want you to go see the property before they share information with you. Remember, they want you to fall in love with the property before you see the numbers. In the beginning, I used to fall for this and spent a lot of time visiting properties that turned out to be lemons. I wasted a lot of time driving around, but it was a good lesson to learn. Nowadays I get the information before I ever drive to the property and end up deciding whether to continue or not.

Here are some of my initial screening questions to find out if the property is something I am interested in. Remember, after you ask a question, you need to be quiet and wait for the answer. Don't put words in their mouths, just be quiet and wait for the answers. It is okay to have a list of questions in front of you to make sure that you get all the information you need.

1) Are all the units occupied? This enables me to find out if I have many vacancies to fill if I take over the property. Filling vacancies can take a long time and therefore be very expensive. Also, if there are many vacancies, I will want to know why. Chances are that the property's condition is run-down or crime has taken over, driving tenants out. In any case, there is a problem that you want addressed.

2) What is the unit mix? I want to know how many studios, 1 bedroom, 2 bedroom and so forth.

3) What is the tenant mix? I want to know if I have many roommate situations or families. Also, if the property is in a college town, I want to know how many units are occupied by students because of big summer vacancies that I may have to contend with. I try to avoid a lot of roommate situations because they tend to have higher vacancies and management problems. For example, tenants in a unit may not like each other, or they may get into a fight and move out. You are left with a situation where the remaining tenants cannot afford to pay rent; you get desperate and rent to someone else quickly because you must get it filled; the existing tenants already have a relationship and they don't like the new tenant. You will have complaint after complaint. In my opinion, I think it is a lot easier to deal with related occupants. If you have studios or one bed rooms, then single tenants will be perfect.

4) How much is rent? You will want to know how much actual rent is collected for each unit type per month. This is the money you will be using to pay for everything.

5) What percentages of tenants pay rent on time? The realtor may not know the answer to this question, but I insist they find out from the seller and get back to me. If you have a situation where half the tenants pay rent after the 15th, you are guaranteed to get into trouble. Your mortgage payments will be due somewhere between the 1st and the 5th of every month and the penalties for paying late are enormous. If I am getting a great deal that may be okay, but you should be aware that it will take time to train your tenants to pay on time. You might have to kick out a few of them to show that you mean business, but this is not cheap or easy. You will have to consult with your team to determine if this is something you want to take on.

6) Are there any pending evictions? Again, the realtor may not have an answer to this question, but I will require that they get this information from the seller. Evictions take time and are very expensive, especially when you have attorneys involved. Personally, if I knew that evictions were under way, I would require the seller to complete them before I took over.

7) Are the leases annual or month-to-month? There are two schools of thought on this one. Some investors prefer month-to-month tenants because they can get them out easier if they cause trouble. Others prefer 6 or 12 month leases because the tenants are tied down to a long term lease. I prefer the annual lease because I have a somewhat stable situation. My thinking is that, if I am worrying that much about getting a tenant out, I do not want them as a tenant to begin with.

8) Who pays which utilities? In master metered buildings, the tenants have no incentive to conserve. I prefer individually metered utilities because tenants pay for their usage. If I have master metered utilities, I work hard to come up with methods to pass the expense to the tenants.

9) Who manages the property? The property manager will have a lot of insights on what works or does not work. If the property is professionally managed, I would not disclose to the manager that I was going to change management. I would want them to believe that they will continue the management so they are upfront with information. If the seller manages by himself then you don't have the same problem.

10) What is the condition of the property, and is there deferred maintenance? You may not get the whole truth here, but you will have a feel for what is going on based on the answer you get. Prod some more if you are not sure what they mean.

11) What improvements have been made recently? With this question I am trying to find out when the water heaters, furnaces, roofs, etc. were updated. Again, don't be shy; ask follow up questions to get a good picture of what is going on.

12) What are the best features about the property? This will give me ideas on how I will market the property if I end up buying it. The more good features the better, but remember to verify anything they tell you. People have a tendency to exaggerate.

13) What are the problems? Every property has problems, but I am hoping to find out what some of them are. I ask how they would solve the problem to give me some ideas from the get go. Some people are so honest and will give you great information that is useful.

14) What is the existing financing on the property and is the loan assumable? I am trying to find out the existing financing to get an idea of how I may structure the deal. If the loan is assumable, you may just be able to take over the loan without the lengthy traditional qualifying. Bear in mind, though, that you have to meet the criteria set by the lenders to assume the loan. You may also find out that the loans are held by private investors, who may be easier and cheaper to work with than a bank.

15) Are the sellers willing to do seller financing? If you are dealing with a seller who has a lot of equity, they may be willing to carry all or part of the contract for you. But you will never know this if you don't ask.

16) How long have they owned the property? If they have owned the property for 25 - 30 years, they may have no mortgages, meaning they may be in a position to carry the contract for you. They will also be in a position to work the terms that may be more favorable to you.

17) How did you arrive at the asking price? In many instances, sellers or realtors set an asking price that is unreasonable, either because they are looking for a sucker or they have no clue what they are doing. Other times it was due to the recommendation of the realtor who promised a higher than realistic asking price to get the listing. I have had some realtors confess that they knew the asking price was too high, but they had to do it because that is what the seller insisted on. When I hear this, I know I may have some cooperation from them.

18) Why are they selling? They may not tell you the truth, but, again, there is no harm in asking. You may get a seller who will spill the beans and give you the ammunition you need to go for a deep

discount. If they tell you that they are moving out of state on a job transfer and they must get rid of the property, you know they are motivated.

19) "Is there anything else you can tell me about the property or the area?" Here you are fishing for more information that they may disclose that may be of benefit to you. I have been surprised how much information people are willing to disclose when you ask them nicely.

20) "I need you to send me the breakdown of income and expenses for the past 2 or 3 years." Some sellers may be uncomfortable with sending me this information, but tell them, "I must know what I am dealing with in order to make a realistic offer." At this point, they may require you to sign a Confidentiality Agreement stating that you will not share the information with anyone other than your advisors. Sign the agreement and get the information.

It is a numbers game

You should have a goal of contacting a certain number of sellers per week based on the results you want. At the beginning this may be scary to you, but remember, it will get easier with time. You have to get over your fear of calling. The worst that can happen is that they will say no. After you are done with your calls, evaluate what you did right or wrong and determine how to improve. If people are being defensive when you ask certain questions, try different ways of asking the same question and find out if you get friendlier responses.

Be pleasant and relaxed when you call. Have your list of questions in front of you to make sure that you cover all your bases. Remember, the more sellers you call the higher the chance of getting someone willing to work with you. Schedule out the time you will call and let nothing get in your way. Things happen, but don't let them get in your way.

The worst they can say is no

Over the years that I have been making offers, nobody has ever thrown something at me. The worst thing that can happen is they say no. You have to understand from the onset that you will hear many more NOs than YESes. With that understanding, go out there and get your NOs out of the way.

Most of the people you are calling are complete strangers and you will never meet them. So what if you think you will sound like an idiot? They don't know you and, in all likelihood, you will never run into them. As I said before, people who win are the ones who just take the NOs and move on. Have fun with this thing. Burn through the NOs quickly and get to the YESes. It gets very exciting when you have a live one to work with.

Letters of Intent

Once you have a deal that sounds workable, you should write a letter of intent. This just states the major deal points like purchase price and other important terms. I will include a template I use which you are welcome to use. This form is for example purposes only and you should check with your attorney before you using it to understand its legal implications. Here is the form I use:

August 10th 20XX

NON-BINDING LETTER OF INTENT

Dear: <u>REALTOR OR SELLER</u>;

This non-binding letter is being written to convey my sincere interest in purchasing the properties located at:

XYZ STREET

ANY TOWN, UT 84XXX

After doing a thorough review of the income and expense information you provided, we are able to make an offer to purchase the property under the terms outlined below:

The purchase price is to be $200,000. We will pay $20,000 down payment and

ask the sellers to carry the remaining $180,000 until July 2010 when the pre-payment penalty expires, at which time we will refinance and pay them off. We will make payments (assuming $1,618.95)on the underlying 1st mortgage. Please review the attached spreadsheet which I used as my basis for our offer.

This offer is based on the fact that the 1st mortgage payment is so high that we will have no return on our investment (ROI) for the first year. I would love to have a discussion with you and the owner about my offer because I think we are being very reasonable given the circumstances.

Offer price is subject to adjustment after all the income and expense information has been verified based on 2007 and 2008 schedule "E" tax returns and year-to-date figures for 2009.

Please let me know if this is acceptable so we can draw up the contract. We look forward to hearing back from you within 72 hours with a favorable response so we can draw up a contract.

This is a non-binding letter of intent to convey interest to purchase property mentioned above. After an agreement on price is reached, a formal legal contract with all the pertinent details on the transaction will be drawn.

Sincerely,

Mati M. Ntongondu
Salama Properties LLC
Investor

This takes me a few minutes to prepare once I have all the numbers. I want to work out the important deal points first before I bother with writing a formal offer. This will save you a lot of expenses and time. You will want to discuss with your realtor and attorney how to handle this.

You should make a goal of sending out at least one letter of intent a week until you get a favorable response. You may have to talk to a few sellers to get to a point of writing a letter of intent, so keep dialing until you get some good leads. Remember this: IF THE OFFER DOES NOT MAKE YOU EMBARRASSED, YOU ARE OFFERING TOO MUCH. If you are having all your offers accepted, you are offering too much. If everything is rejected, you may be onto something. Be reasonable, but remember, you can never offer lower once you mention a higher price.

The Formal Offer

After you have an agreement based on the Letter of Intent you presented, the next step is to make the formal offer. Once an offer is accepted, it becomes a legally binding document with consequences for not completing your end of the deal. Work with your realtor or attorney to make sure that you include contingency clauses that will enable you to back out without losing your earnest money or getting sued for specific performance. The following is a list of clauses that I use on my offers. Remember, these are presented for example purposes only and you are advised to work with your realtor and/or attorney to determine what is appropriate for your situation.

1. Seller to provide inventory of all personal property by Seller Disclosure Deadline.

2. Seller to provide an accounting (by apartment unit) of all the security deposits by Seller Disclosure Deadline. Deposits to be transferred to the buyer at settlement.

3. Sale contingent upon approval of buyer's attorney.

4. Seller to provide to buyer the filled out TENANT QUESTIONNAIRES by Seller Disclosure Deadline. Blank questionnaires to be provided by buyer.

5. Seller to disclose and provide the documentation of all service contracts that do not expire by settlement deadline by Seller Disclosure Deadline.

6. All rents to be pro-rated as of the day of settlement whether collected or otherwise.

7. Sale is contingent upon inspection and approval of all units which shall be in rent-ready condition at settlement.

8. Seller to provide "SCHEDULE-E" for 3 previous tax years by Seller Disclosure Deadline.

9. Seller to provide "RENT ROLLS" and a "PROFIT AND LOSS" for the property for 3 previous tax years by Seller Disclosure Deadline.

10. Seller to provide all account numbers for utilities by Seller Disclosure Deadline. All utility deposits to be transferred to buyer at settlement.

11. Seller to provide all unexpired warranty information for any work done to the property or appliances by Seller Disclosure Deadline.

12. Sale contingent upon approval by partner(s).

13. Offer price subject to adjustment based on review of verifiable 3 previous years' income and expenses information.

14. Seller shall provide to buyer written warranty of the property for two years after settlement against termite and any other pest infestation. Seller shall bear all costs for extermination and eradication of such infestations.

15. Seller or agent to show the buyer or buyer's agent all maintenance issues relating to the property before Evaluations and Inspections Deadline.

16. Buyer may ask any questions about the property and is due answers from the seller to the best of his/her knowledge in a timely manner.

This is a long list of contingencies and I make it long on purpose. I have never had a seller agree to all of them, but invariably they will counter on one or more. When I acquiesce to their counter offer, they feel as if I am giving up on something, and they are more likely to be more cooperative. In reality, I may not care about getting some of the contingencies I use, but it enables me to barter for something important that I want.

Chapter 10: THE DUE DILIGENCE

This is the time that you distinguish the truth from fiction. I make sure that I receive all the documents mentioned in the last chapter under the heading The Formal Offer.

I go over all the leases and make sure that the rental income information I got from the seller is the same as what is shown on the leases. Whatever is listed on the leases is what you must abide by. I check that the amount of security deposits information is also corroborated by what is showing on the leases.

I check on the expiration dates on the leases to make sure that I don't have a majority of leases expiring in the same month. If this is the case, I must figure out a strategy to handle the potential problem. If, on the other hand, I rent to college students, then it is okay that most of my leases expire in August, because I know it will be easy to rent units for the fall semester. No matter what it is, you just have to be aware and have a strategy to manage the situation. If you don't have a strategy, you may be in a world of hurt.

I look at the seller's 'Schedule E' portion of their tax returns and other financials to make sure that they correspond to the numbers I used to arrive at my offer. I use the income and expense information they reported to Uncle Sam. I would not take the word of a seller who claimed that they fudged the numbers on their taxes. If the new figures are different and I end up needing to lower my offer price, I just do it. If the seller does not like it, I bid him farewell and move on.

Next I plan for inspection of the property. This means walking each and every unit with a general contractor who can give me input on the spot on what I am seeing. If you don't have a friend who will do this with you for free or for the price of lunch, it will be a good investment to pay someone to go with you, unless, of course, you are a general contractor yourself. I have seen some incredible things during the walk through, including apartments full of garbage which you can't walk though. If all is well, I will then hire an inspector to look everything over in detail. This is not free, but it is money well spent.

Next I send out Tenant Questionnaires (for smaller complexes) to be filled out by the seller and the tenants. This is how I make sure that the seller is telling me the truth. For example, if the seller states that the tenant paid $400 for their security deposit, and the tenant puts down that they paid $200, I know I have a discrepancy that must be resolved. I get information from these questionnaires that may not be reflected in the leases. You have to remember that, once you take over the property, you will own all the good and the bad. For example, I have uncovered information such as sellers stating that they don't allow pets, but have the tenant put down that they have two dogs. I have included the two questionnaires I use. As stated before, these are for example purposes only and you must check with your attorney before using such forms.

Note that I do all the checking myself, regardless whether I have an attorney/ agent. Nobody will care about your deal more than you.

Part of my due diligence involves walking around to talk to the neighbors to find out what kind of problems the property has. I am mainly interested in knowing if there is criminal activity that I need to be aware of. Neighbors are very willing to disclose information on drug activity, fights, and any other issues. I also visit the nearby police station and get their input on the crime activity in the area.

I visit with the City Planning and Zoning Departments and introduce myself as an investor in the process of buying a property in their city. I ask them for any new road construction, the number of multi-family dwellings approved to be built, and what the trends are for the area. I also get information on new companies moving into the area and about ones moving out. These departments are a wealth of information and are very willing to help. Just remember to think through what they are telling you and ask follow up questions if the information does not make sense.

I call all the utility companies and verify that the information offered by the seller is accurate. If any of the companies will not give me the information, I contact the owner to call them and authorize the release of the information to me. I try to work out an equal pay plan for gas and electricity where possible to avoid the seasonal highs and lows which make budgeting difficult.

TENANT QUESTIONNAIRE

To be completed by tenant/Ser llenado por arrendatario)

Tenant name(s)/ *Nombre de arrendatario*: _____

Home Phone/*Llame en casa*: _____

E-Mail/*correo electrónico*: _____

Employer/Empleador: _____ Address/*Dirección*: _____

_____

_____ Phone/*trabaje teléfono*: _____

How many live in the apartment/*Cuántos vivo en el appartment*: _____

How long have you lived here/*Cuán largo ha vivido usted aquí*: _____

How much rent do you pay/*Cuánto alquiler paga usted*: _____

How much deposit did you pay/*Cuánto depósito pagó usted*: _____

What date of month do you pay rent/*Qué fecha de de mes paga usted el alquiler*: _____

How many pets do you own/Cuántos animales favoritos posee usted: _____

What kind of pets/ *Qué clase de animales favoritos*: _____

_____

Does any furniture belong to owner/ *Pertenece cualquier muebles al propietario*: _____

_____

_____

Do you have any special arrangements with owner/manager/ *Tiene usted algún arreglo especial con propietario*: _____

_____

_____

_____

_____

Notes/ *Notas*: _____

Signature/*Firma*   Date/*Fecha*

_____   _____

TENANT QUESTIONNAIRE
(To be completed by seller/manager)

Tenant name(s): _____, _____

Employer of record: _____ Address: _____

_____ Phone: _____

Is tenant current on rent: _____

What day of month does tenant pay rent: _____

How many times in the past 6 months has tenant paid late: _____

How many times have you served a 3-day notice to tenant: _____

Is tenant a nuisance to other tenants: _____

_____

_____

*** Please let me know what else you think I should know about the tenant:

_____

_____

_____

_____

*** PLEASE LET ME KNOW YOUR HONEST OPINION OF THE TENANT.
I WOULD GREATLY APPRECIATE A COPY OF THE RENTAL APPLICATION THE
TENANT(S) FILLED OUT WHEN THEY MOVED IN.

Signature/Date

_____/_____

Chapter 11: FINDING THE MONEY

Find the deal and money will come

If there is one idea I want to impress on you very firmly, it is that, when you have a killer deal, money will show up. It took me a few years for this to sink in. I would prepare great presentations and sit down with people who I was sure had money to share my in wonderful plans, but they all said NO. Let's face it, successful people are not stupid, otherwise they wouldn't be successful. They get approached by many people with all sorts of business ideas looking for funding and turn most of them down.

I was getting frustrated, but I kept reading that you have to find the deals and money will follow. In my mind, I had to have the money lined up before I found the deal, but I was doing it all wrong. I had to take a leap of faith and try the idea out. It was like night and day. I have to admit that it scared me to death to put an apartment listing under contract when I did not know where the money was going to come from. I had a tough time coming up with the earnest money for the deal.

Once I had my first deal under contract, everything changed. I could not believe that I had accomplished such a feat. I had an amazing deal and I knew it. It gave me great confidence to go out there and talk to people about it. I knew that I had struck gold when one investor offered me $50,000 to assign the contract to him. It was extremely hard to say no to the offer, but this meant I had to close the deal one way or another. I presented the deal to a few people, and everybody wanted in. I had proven, beyond any shadow of a doubt, that money would follow after I found the deal.

Let the deal do the talking

As discussed above, once you have a good deal, you don't have to hard sell it to raise the money needed to close. Sit down with the correct people and present the numbers in a simple way that makes sense and magic happens. They start asking you questions and selling themselves on the deal.

Don't expect everybody to say yes to your offer. It will not be the right timing for some people, but, if there is interest, get permission to call them down the road with information on subsequent deals. Also don't take it as a personal rejection when some people say no. If someone says no to you, just move on to the next. Chances are that you will be so excited you will be ready to move on because, after all, you have something of value to offer them.

Sphere of influence & Growing your network

The best place to start is with people you know. If you are educated and know what you are talking about, they will listen to you. Work on expanding your sphere of influence by asking them who they know who has money. Keep your list growing and, before long, you will have a network of people to take deals to.

Another excellent place to pick up potential partners is at your local investors' club. Work on networking with fellow investors and get the names of people they know who have money to invest in good real estate.

Write and practice your dialogue so it flows naturally when you talk to people. Be sure to introduce yourself as a real estate investor, and always ask people if they are interested in investing in good deals. I have heard it said that a majority of people would like to invest in real estate if they knew how to do it and had the means. There are people looking to invest, and if you don't approach them and tell them what you do, they will never know.

The topic of raising money is so important that I am constantly studying how other people do it. Let's face it, you have to be able to raise the capital for your deals if you are ever to close them. If you have some successful methods that have worked very well for you, please let me know so I can share with others. My email address is mati@salamaproperties.com

Chapter 12: MANAGING THE PROPERTY

Bad management ruins good investments

Bad management can ruin the best property investment in town. Unlike purchasing a property, which is a short exercise, property management is long term and it is a 24-7 job. I have heard it said that property investing would be fun if there were no people involved. People who talk like this are missing the point. They forget that, without the people to pay the mortgage, they would have to make the payments out of their pocket.

Property management is people intensive, and, if you don't like dealing with people, you better hire a manager because you will get sick of it pretty quickly. You have to have the right mentality if you want to be in the business of property management. First off, you have to stop thinking of your tenants as an annoyance but as a big blessing because they pay your mortgage.

Second, you have to come to terms with the fact that this job is 24-7 and that you have to take care of problems in a timely manner. If you ignore tenants' issues, you will have none very soon, and you will be the type of motivated seller who investors are looking for.

What is involved in management?

As I have stated above, management is a 24-7 job. Managers are always on call. Here are some of the jobs that a property manager has to do:

1) Marketing. When you have vacancies you will have to market to get them filled. Research the most efficient ways to market your property.

2) Showing units. After you market the property, you will get calls and will need to show the property to potential tenants. You have to be flexible on showing times, because people will not always conform to your schedule.

3) Applicant screening. After you show the property and get someone interested in renting, you will have to screen them to make sure that they are tenants you are willing to rent to. Remember that over 90% of

the problems with management can be avoided by proper screening. I would not dream of renting to anyone without a credit and background check. It is very costly to kick a bad tenant out once they have taken occupancy.

4) Leasing vacant units. After screening and finding the correct tenant, you will go over all the appropriate forms and have them sign them before you allow them to move in.

5) Rent collection. At the end of every month, you will collect rent. This can be collected by someone onsite or you can have rents mailed to you. If I have to have rents mailed, I always want them to go to a P.O. Box instead of my home. I would never want tenants bringing rent to my home because of security concerns.

6) Bill payment for all utilities & services. You will keep track of and pay for all utilities in a timely manner. There is nothing more annoying to tenants than having their electricity or gas turned off when they have paid their rent on time. If you think about it, it is very inconsiderate of you to willfully have this happen. You may want to have these paid by direct deposit or have some reminders to make sure that you pay utilities on time.

7) Developing & enforcing community policies & rules. If you have a multi-unit property, you will have to come up with rules to both protect your property and tenants from one another. Here is a sample of community rules and policies I have developed for my properties:

COMMUNITY POLICIES AND RULES

Dear valued tenant,

We have these rules to promote a cohesive and an orderly community that functions for the enjoyment and safety of all. These policies and rules are put together in a spirit of good will, not to make anybody's life difficult. If there are issues that you may want to see addressed to enhance our community atmosphere, please contact the manager with your suggestions.

A. There will be a $5.00 charge for each lost key.

B. Cats or other animals will not be allowed in or on the premises or grounds at any time whether permanent or temporary, whether belonging to the residents or guests, without first obtaining written management approval.

C. There will be no smoking in the apartment by residents or guests. Any resident who smokes or allow guests to smoke in their unit automatically assumes the expense of re-painting and cleaning of the carpets. The Utah Clean Air Act restricts smoking from within 25ft of the doorways. Cigarette butts must be deposited in the correct receptacles located by the building entrances.

D. All items that are not the personal property of the residents or their guests are to remain within the apartment or in the common areas at all times. Only management is authorized to remove them. There shall be no tampering with screens, TV antennas, electrical systems or any other fixtures or systems.

E. Gasoline, fireworks or other combustible materials are not to be stored on the premises. Nothing shall be stored in the furnace rooms as they could be a fire hazard.

F. There are to be no waterbeds without the written approval of management.

G. Automobiles, motorcycles, bicycles or other mechanical equipment may be driven or parked only in designated areas, never on common areas. There shall be no major repairs or dissembling on the premises. Any inoperable equipment will be removed at the owner's expense. Due to limited parking space, each unit is allowed to park only one car. It is the tenant's responsibility to keep their parking area clean.

H. No party shall violate any local, state, or national laws or health code.

I. Engagement in any criminal activity will be reported to the police and will constitute grounds for eviction and forfeiture of security deposit. Disorderly conduct which disturbs the peace or any activities creating a nuisance or endangering the health and safety of individuals or damaging property is strictly prohibited.

J.   Rent is due on the 1st of each month. There shall be a $20 late fee and a $30 per day delinquency fee after the 3rd. If rent is not received by 5:00 pm on the 3rd, a Three Day Notice to Pay Rent or Quit notice will be served promptly and the eviction process will commence.

K.   The manager shall give the tenant 2 written warnings to rectify a situation causing a nuisance or violating the lease. If the tenant does not remedy the situation, they shall be given the appropriate notice which requires compliance or the eviction process will begin.

L.   Residents agree to inform management of any occurrence of disturbing, destructive, hazardous, unlawful or suspicious activities on or near the premises and management agree to strictly enforce the policies and rules according to its best judgment.

M.   No nails, screws, or adhesive hangers, except standard picture hooks, shade brackets, and curtain rod brackets, may be placed on walls, woodwork, or any part of the apartment.

N.   Entrances, walkways, and driveways shall not be obstructed or used for any purpose other than ingress and egress.

O.   Tenant is prohibited from adding locks, changing, or in any way altering locks installed on the doors. All keys must be returned to management of the premises upon termination of occupancy.

P.   In consideration of the quiet enjoyment of residents who live in close proximity to the laundry room, the hours of operation for the laundry machines will be between 8:00 am to 9:30 pm.

Q.   All maintenance work, including painting, must be done by or delegated by the on-site managers. Residents are not authorized to do any work on the apartments without prior written consent of management. There will be NO REIMBURSMENTS given to tenants who do work without authorization.

R. All maintenance requests shall be made using the MAINTENACE REQUEST FORMS located _____
_____. Emergency maintenance requests should be made either by calling the managers or by contacting them at their apartment to expedite the handling of the requests. In case of fire or other life threatening emergencies, please call the police or 911. Please be respectful of the manager's time and privacy.

S. The following is the cleaning checklist you may use when you vacate the apartment to ensure that you have your SECURITY DEPOSIT returned to you:

- ✓ REMOVE FINGERPRINTS AND MARKS FROM WALLS, DOORS, AND DOOR FRAMES

- ✓ CLEAN WALL LIGHT FIXTURES AND WINDOW PANES

- ✓ CLEAN STOVE AND OVEN, INCLUDING INSIDE OVEN, OVERHEAD HOOD, FILTER, DRIP PANS, RIMS, AND AREA UNDERNEATH DRIP PANS

- ✓ EMPTY AND CLEAN INSIDE REFRIGERATOR/FREEZER. WIPE DOWN EXTERIOR. CLEAN OUTSIDE AND INSIDE ALL CABINETS

- ✓ CLEAN SINK AND COUNTERTOPS

- ✓ SCRUB KITCHEN AND BATHROOM FLOORS. VACUUM THE CARPETS

- ✓ CLEAN TOILET, SINK, CABINETS, AND SHOWER

Please give us your comments on what we can do to make XXXXXX Apartments a better community. Feel free to contact Chris at XXX-XXX-XXXXX with suggestions. We would love to hear from you.

Tenant(s) has read and accepts these Community Policies and Rules

_____   _____   _____   _____
Tenant Signature   Date   Tenant Signature   Date

8) Coordinating evictions. Once in a while you may have to deal with evicting a tenant for non payment of rent or for other breach of lease. You have to learn how to do this yourself or hire an attorney to take care of it.

9) Continuously evaluate ways to reduce cost and increase income. Management is about reducing costs and increasing income. Don't be a cheapskate and forget to take care of your tenants in the name of reducing costs. If you do this, you will pay with increased vacancies. As you manage more effectively, you will increase your property's value.

10) 24/7 Emergency response. You are on call at all times. If you ignore tenants' calls in the middle of the night, you may pay dearly when you call back in the morning only to find out that there is massive water damage which could have been taken care of easily had you answered your phone.

11) Move-in and move-out inspections. When tenants move in, you will need to do a move in inspection; you will have to do a move out inspection when they leave. This will enable you to see if there is tenant caused damage that they will have to pay for.

12) Maintenance. Depending on your fixing skills, you will do some maintenance work or hire it out to professionals when things break. In older buildings, you should plan on having many plumbing issues like leaky faucets. You should think twice before you handle major plumbing issues, electrical, or HVAC problems unless you have the skills to do it.

13) Record keeping. Management is intensive on bookkeeping. Sometimes you will wonder if you are in the bookkeeping or management business. This must be done right because you have to report the property operations come tax time.

Should you manage your own property or hire it out

After seeing the long list of duties a property manager has to do, you may be saying this is not for you. If this seems too much for you to handle, don't worry because you can hire a management company to take care of all of this for you. If you are the type of person who is soft and wants to empathize with every sob story, then please don't manage your property by yourself. The fact of the matter is that tenants lie, and you will hear very creative stories.

If you decide to hire a property manager, make sure that they have experience in managing properties similar to yours. Shop around for a good manager and ask for referrals. Don't just hire the first guy or girl you come across.

Conclusion

Real estate investing is fun and profitable, but you need to know what you are doing. It requires specialized knowledge, but you don't have to have all this knowledge yourself, you just need to know enough to direct a team of professionals to attain your goal.

Before you buy any property, you need to have a goal on how you will manage it. Management is long term and time consuming. You will need to have the correct attitude about your tenants if you choose to manage by yourself. You have to see them as your customers who can put you out of business if you do not take care of them. Happy investing.

- A LITTLE ABOUT ME -

I was born and raised in a small village in Kenya, the oldest of 7 children. I moved to the U.S. in 1991 to go to college with intentions of going back to Kenya after my studies. I met and married my beautiful wife Colleen at Brigham Young University (BYU) in Provo, Utah and decided to settle down and have a family.

I graduated from BYU in 1997 with a master's degree in civil engineering and worked for a consulting firm in the California's San Francisco Bay area and then for the State of Utah as an engineer. The apartment ownership seed was planted in me when my wife and I took a job as on-site apartment managers in California to make ends meet. I was the fix-it man, and she was the bookkeeper. This was a tough job, but I noticed that the landlord would always call us from Pebble Beach and other exotic places to check on rent collection. I decided that one day, I would be the owner, with managers to call.

When we moved back to Utah in 1999, I got my real estate and mortgage licenses and started working in both professions part time. After a few months, I started Personal Advantage Mortgage and had a great time doing loans and networking with people in the field. During my time as a mortgage broker, I was surprised at the lack of financial literacy that plagued even the very educated consumer. At the same time, I was also working as a Realtor and learning how to put real estate deals together.

I started Salama Properties, LLC in 2006 to acquire and manage properties for myself and other investors. It has been very rewarding to own apartments and be on the other side of the equation as a landlord with managers I call to check on rent collection. This is just the beginning of the journey for me and I am working on owning many apartment buildings with many managers to call while I am visiting exotic places. After getting several mentorship requests from aspiring investors, I decided to write this book to aid in my teaching.

I hope the material you have read in this book will inspire you to take action. I have heard one smart investor say that if all you do is buy courses and books and do not take action on what you are studying, you will end up with a very smart book collection. Please let me know what you think of the material covered. I would also greatly appreciate you sharing any money raising ideas that have worked for you. Please send your comments to me at: mati@salamaproperties.com

Sincerely,
Mati M. Ntongondu

Mati M. Ntongondu
P.O. Box 41
Helotes, TX 78023
mati@salamaproperties.com